ADVENT WOMEN
FROM EVE
TO MARY

ADVENT WOMEN
FROM EVE TO MARY

Lyn Fraser

Advent Women from Eve to Mary
Copyright © 2017 Lyn Fraser

CrossLink Publishing
www.crosslinkpublishing.com

All rights reserved. No part of this book may be reproduced in any form, except for brief quotations in reviews, without the written permission of the author.

Printed in the United States of America. All rights reserved under International Copyright Law.

ISBN 978-1-63357-111-2

Library of Congress Control Number: 2017939153

All scriptures are taken from the New Revised Standard Version Bible, copyright © 1989 the Division of Christian Education of the National Council of the Churches of Christ in the United States of America. Used by permission. All rights reserved.

Cover Art, Mary Southard, CSJ

For Reenie and Jasper

TABLE OF CONTENTS

INTRODUCTION
    DEVOTION AND CELEBRATION 1
IN THE BEGINNING
    EVE 7
    SARAH 13
    REBEKAH 18
THE RISK-TAKERS
    TAMAR 25
    MIRIAM 31
    RAHAB 35
THE BOLD ONES
    DEBORAH 41
    RUTH 45
    ESTHER 51
THE INCARNATION
    ELIZABETH 57
    MARY 63
    REFERENCES 71

INTRODUCTION

Devotion and Celebration

Advent, which is celebrated by Christians as the special period encompassing four Sundays before Christmas, is a season of hope and expectation. It is a time for quiet preparation as we await the momentous intersection of the divine and human in Jesus' birth. Advent is my personal favorite season of the church calendar. I appreciate the emphasis on quietness, on spiritual centering and preparation, on lighting candles and singing softly. But Advent can also be a season of confusion. This time of waiting brings with it an awareness of how our faith and sense of hope affect our actions in the world as we confront a secular swirl with emphasis on the material aspects of life. For some, the days before and after Christmas are ones of acute emotional pain, of depression and guilt and sadness.

Holy scriptures engage this tension: the potential for experiencing deep darkness in what we are told through societal expectations is a season of great light and merriment. Taking some time each day to read and reflect on the scriptural stories of God's interaction with the faithful people of biblical history is a way to enlighten our personal and communal advents, these seasons of wonder that are roiled by the potential for doubt and confusion.

My own family's spiritual practice during the Advent season for many years has been the tradition of the tree of Jesse, which uses daily readings from scripture to trace our relationship with God from creation in Genesis, through Jesus' birth in the New Testament. Accompanying each day's reading is a symbol to place on or under a live tree reflecting that day's content, so that by Christmas Day the Jesse Tree is laden with or surrounded by objects, such as fruit, stars, a rainbow, birds, work animals, a ladder, angels, tools, and a baby in the manger.

Most of the daily readings come from the Old Testament, emphasizing God's promises through the lineage of its patriarchs from Abraham to Isaac to Jacob, and on to David. The symbol of the Jesse Tree itself is taken from the passage in Isaiah, "A shoot shall come out from the stump of Jesse, and a branch shall grow out of his roots" (11:1). This verse about Jesse, father of David, speaks of new growth in David's lineage.

Although the narrative focuses on the patriarchal lineage to Jesus, it has become increasingly obvious from reading these same passages year after year how important the lesser-known women are to this story. The female characters give birth to subsequent generations, but they do *so much more* than procreate. Not always virtuous, these women of Advent are endlessly creative, wonderfully adventuresome, necessarily defiant, occasionally manipulative, and absolutely essential to the biblical narrative.

Eve, for instance, has gotten quite a bad rap in post-biblical discourse. The original matriarch and maternal archetype, her concerns are for nurture and sustenance. While Eve makes mistakes—eating fruit forbidden to Adam and blaming the serpent—there's much more to her story than alleged sin and seduction.

Sarah laughs at the very notion she will bear a child at the age of 90. Talk about hope. But she later laughs *with* God, in joy, and along the way stirs up plenty of trouble while saving Abraham's life at least twice.

Within just one dramatic scene, **Rebekah**—wife of Isaac, mother of Esau and Jacob—determines the entire course of her family's future.

In a chapter of Genesis that we never read in church, **Tamar** allows herself to be viewed as a 'woman of the street.' All the while, she's just following Israelite law and her commitment to God.

Miriam, sister of Moses, is well known for protecting him as an infant, thus ensuring his safety in Pharaoh's household and ultimate leadership of his people. She is lesser known as the first female prophet in Hebrew scripture, as a partner in leadership with Moses and Aaron, as an outcast supported by her people, and for a musical legacy that extends to the psalms.

The prostitute, **Rahab,** outsmarts the king's men in Jericho, saving Joshua's spies and helping ensure his eventual victory.

Deborah, the only female judge in Hebrew scripture and also a prophet, is a decisive figure in Israel's defeat of the Canaanites.

Radical, faithful, risk-taking **Ruth** challenges the conventions of her society while successfully living within it.

Queen Esther uses wits and political savvy to save her exiled people from destruction at the hands of their enemies.

Elizabeth, like Sarah, barren until late in life, rejoices in her conception, the child in her womb leaping with joy, and demonstrates faith while her husband is struck dumb for not believing. She provides encouragement and a lengthy period of shelter to her young cousin **Mary,** who magnifies God in celebration of her own pregnancy, ultimately giving birth in a place shared with animals. Mary mothers her son Jesus from the beginning to the end of his ministry, watching him die on the cross and joining others in the early prayers of Christianity.

Without these women, there would be no Advent. It is through their stories that we witness the momentous event we anticipate as each woman experiences and responds to the presence of God in her very human life.

Intrigued and stirred by these stories, my family's observance has shifted its emphasis to include a celebration of these women. Each day during Advent, we read and reflect on the scriptural narratives–beginning with creation and tracing God's revelations and interactions through Mary's birthing and mothering of Jesus. Honoring some aspect of each woman's journey, we place one or more symbols on or by the plant, joining the symbols we've used through the years in the tradition of Jesse's tree.

As a guide for others who would like to follow a spiritual practice that includes a focus on these women of Advent, I am providing the scriptural references for each woman, an introductory passage from scripture, a narrative discussion (not a scholarly study) of the woman's life based on scripture, suggestions for symbols, and questions for reflection. The translation used is the *New Revised Standard Version*, but the full scriptural references are provided so that a reader can select from any personal choice of translation. Based on the scripture, narrative, and suggested questions, readers can also use this material for daily individual study and for group discussion.

The organization of material in this book is based on the order in which each woman's story appears in the biblical narrative and is divided into suggested weekly sections that correspond to the four Sundays of Advent:

First Sunday of Advent: In the Beginning: Eve, Sarah, Rebekah
Second Sunday of Advent: The Risk-Takers: Tamar, Miriam, Rahab
Third Sunday of Advent: The Bold Ones: Deborah, Ruth, Esther
Fourth Sunday of Advent: The Incarnation: Elizabeth and Mary

Through reading and reflecting on these very human stories we discover not only their experiences of faith, but the potential for our own.

Note on the Advent Calendar: Advent always includes the four Sundays before Christmas, but the actual number of days depends on the day of the week on which Christmas occurs. Readers can begin a weekly spiritual practice on the first Sunday of Advent and continue on the second, third, and fourth Sundays, possibly adjusting for the varying length of the last week.

EVE

Scriptural References: Genesis 2, 3 and 4

Now the serpent was more crafty than any other wild animal that the Lord had made. He said to the woman, "Did God say, 'You shall not eat from any tree in the garden?'" The woman said to the serpent, "We may eat of the fruit of the trees in the garden; but God said, 'You shall not eat of the fruit of the tree that is in the middle of the garden, nor shall you touch it, or you shall die.'" But the serpent said to the woman, "You will not die; for God knows that when you eat of it your eyes will be opened, and you will be like God, knowing good and evil." So when the woman saw that the tree was good for food, and that it was a delight to the eyes, and that the tree was to be desired to make one wise, she took of its fruit and ate; and she also gave some to her husband, who was with her, and he ate. Then the eyes of both were opened, and they knew that they were naked; and they

sewed fig leaves together and made loin cloths for themselves.

They heard the sound of the Lord God walking in the garden at the time of the evening breeze.... "Have you eaten from the tree of which I commanded you not to eat?" The man said, "The woman whom you gave to be with me, she gave me fruit from the tree, and I ate." Then the Lord God said to the woman, "What is this you have done?" The woman said, "The serpent tricked me, and I ate." The Lord God said to the serpent, "Because you have done this, cursed are you among all animals and among all wild creatures." (Genesis 3:1-8, 11-14)

Eve's entire story appears in Chapters 2-4 of Genesis. The cast and setting are familiar: God, Eve, Adam, serpent, garden of Eden. After the serpent succeeds in persuading Eve to eat the 'forbidden fruit,' she shares it with Adam, and off they go on the road to ruin. God responds with wrath and punishments. Ultimately, Adam and Eve propagate humankind.

Much of Eve's iconic reputation turns on a significant conversation she has with the serpent in which she refers to the instructions God had given Adam not to eat from the tree in the middle of the garden. The serpent convinces Eve that it's all right with God, to go ahead and have some of the fruit. Consuming the fruit will make her godlike, the serpent assures Eve; her eyes will be opened, and she will know good and evil.

When Eve sees that the tree is for food, that the food is a delight to the eyes and will instill wisdom, she eats it. As a nurturer, she shares the food with her husband. Sure enough, their eyes are opened: they see one another naked. After sewing fig leaves together and making loin cloths for themselves, they hear from God, perhaps expecting approval. But instead, God admonishes them for eating the forbidden fruit.

The blame game. Adam immediately blames Eve for giving him the fruit from the tree: *Her fault*. Eve, who is not exactly a model of taking responsibility, blames the serpent for tricking her into eating: *Serpent's fault*. Although Adam and Eve get their fair share of wrath, God speaks to the serpent about consequences: *because you have done this*.

God deals with Eve and Adam by giving them work to do. Eve is to bear children, an outcome of desire for her husband, and God tells her the childbearing process will be painful. Adam is to toil all the days of his life.

As the story continues beyond the above excerpt, Adam names his wife Eve "because she was the mother of all living" (Genesis 3:20). She conceives and bears her first son, Cain, saying "I have produced a man with the help of the Lord" (Genesis 4:1), and in this way Eve is presented as a *co-creator* with God of the next generation.

Eve gives birth to another son, Abel, and as the boys grow, Cain becomes jealous of what he perceives to be God's favoring of Abel. God tells Cain, "If you do not do well, sin is lurking at the door" (Genesis 4:6). The first actual reference to 'sin' in scripture is about sibling rivalry and Cain's murdering Abel. Eve subsequently bears a third son, Seth, about whom she says, "God has appointed for me another child instead of Abel, because Cain killed him" (Genesis 4:25).

Eve, the maternal archetype, is a complex character. Human, yes. She eats the fruit that God has commanded Adam not to eat and blames her behavior on the serpent. But as the story shows, her concern is with sustenance and nurture. It is only when she sees that the tree is good for food that she eats and shares the abundance. Her actions also have an essential spiritual objective, making her our first theologian in the understanding of good and evil.God recognizes the source of the disobeying. Who has caused this? The gender-neutral serpent. Subsequently, *sin* raises its head not with Eve, but with Cain.

Through the Genesis story, Eve represents nurture, life, and co-creation with God. As Adam himself points out (Genesis 3:20), Eve is the mother of all living.

Symbols: fruit (biblical scholars think not an apple, possibly a grape, but any fruit is a symbol of fruit), figs and fig leaves, a garden with trees, a woman, a man, and a serpent, an artist's rendering of Eve

Questions for reflection:

What are Eve's particular qualities as the maternal archetype?

What does it mean for this archetypical mother to feature elements that are both light and dark? And grey? How is she like and unlike your own mother? How is she like and unlike you?

What can we learn from Eve about mothering?

What do you think of God's response to Eve, Adam, and the serpent?

Is your impression of Eve changed by reading the full scriptural story, and if so how?

What do you think you would do in the same Garden of Eden situation?

How does Eve embody the Advent theme of hope?

SARAH

Scriptural References: Genesis 11, 12, 16, 17, 18, 20, 21, 23, 24, 25, 49

They said to him, "Where is your wife Sarah?" And he said, "There, in the tent." Then one said, "I will surely return to you in due season, and your wife Sarah shall have a son." And Sarah was listening at the tent entrance behind him. Now Abraham and Sarah were old, advanced in age; it had ceased to be with Sarah after the manner of women. So Sarah laughed to herself, saying, "After I have grown old, and my husband is old, shall I have pleasure?" The Lord said to Abraham, "Why did Sarah laugh, and say, 'Shall I indeed bear a child, now that I am old?' Is anything too wonderful for the Lord? At the set time I will return to you, in due season, and Sarah shall have a son." But Sarah denied, saying, "I did not laugh"; for she was afraid. He said, "Oh yes, you did laugh." (Genesis 18: 9-15)

Barren for 90 years and well beyond the age of fertility, Sarah overhears a message from God to Abraham that she will bear a son. Sarah's response? She laughs. For good reason: she and Abraham are both too old for such outcomes.

We learn about Sarah–wife of Abraham, mother of Isaac, and laugher at God in Genesis. Necessarily tough and self-protective as the matriarch of a tribe frequently on the move, she deals with the challenges that confront her in controversial ways. But in an era when women had little power or even a place in recorded history, Sarah ultimately endures as a figure of hope, as one chosen by God to experience an incomparable miracle. Through it all, God is unwaveringly faithful to her.

Sarah is praised in scripture for obeying her husband. Although she consistently demonstrates fierce loyalty to Abraham in upholding his heritage, we find instances in these chapters where Abraham's obedience leads to complex problems for both of them and for their legacy.

Named Sarai and Abram when we enter the story (Genesis 11:29), God commands that they leave their home in Haran, the first of many moves, and travel to Canaan, where Abram is promised an heir. A famine in Canaan forces the couple to move on to Egypt.

As they are about to enter the country as aliens, Abram acknowledges to Sarai his fear that because of her beauty, the Pharaoh will have him killed and take Sarai for himself. Abram asks that Sarai say she is his sister, not his wife, and Sarai agrees in order to protect Abram. She is taken into Pharaoh's house. In return Abram is given sheep, oxen, donkeys, slaves, and camels. Unfortunately for Pharaoh, God afflicts him with plagues because he's with Sarai, a married woman. In order to end the plagues, Pharaoh releases Sarai back to Abram, and they are once again on their way.

Over the next ten years their overriding disappointment is Sarai's barrenness. Sarai believes she has been prevented from bearing children by God. In deep sadness, she feels the responsibility of God's promising Abram an heir and suggests to Abram that he take up a relationship with her servant Hagar in order to fulfill the promise. Abram listens to Sarai and accepts the gift of Hagar, who conceives. Following the conception, however, Hagar turns on Sarai and treats her with contempt. In response, Sarai deals harshly with her, causing Hagar to run away. Hagar returns to the household only through God's intervention and bears Abram a son, Ishmael.

Things change dramatically for Sarai and Abram when he reaches the age of 99, including the names by which they are known: Abram becomes Abraham and Sarai, Sarah. God blesses Abraham, promising him descendants and land. Three days after this blessing, messengers of God come to Abraham's tent. After he invites them in, Sarah leaves to prepare refreshment for their guests, and one of the men announces that Sarah, now age 90, will have a child in one year.

We know Sarah's response to overhearing that prediction.

Before the prophecy can be fulfilled, however, Sarah and Abraham take yet another trip, this one to Gerar, which is ruled by King Abimelech. The scenario that had occurred in Egypt is repeated. King Abimelech, overwhelmed by Sarah's stunning beauty, wants her for his own wife, which would mean eliminating Abraham as the existing husband. In order to spare his life, Abraham claims Sarah is his sister, not his wife. We learn in this iteration that Sarah is, in fact, the daughter of Abraham's father, but not the daughter of his mother, so she is his half-sister. Before the unfolding of any sex favors, God comes to King Abimelech in a dream and reveals that Sarah is Abraham's wife. Like the Egyptian Pharaoh before him, the king gives Sarah back to Abraham along with many gifts, and the family moves on, encouraged by Abimelech to live anywhere in his land they desire.

A year later, God does for Sarah as promised. Sarah conceives and bears a son. Abraham names him Isaac, which means 'he laughs.' Now Sarah says, "God has brought laughter for me; everyone who hears will laugh with me" (Genesis 21:6). In this instance, the laughter is in joy rather than shocked disbelief.

Sarah herself nurses Isaac, not a wet nurse, and he grows. On the day he is weaned, the family celebrates with a feast, during which Sarah observes something in the play of the two boys, Isaac and the much older Ishmael. What she sees isn't explained—whether it is some kind of abuse or just boys' teasing—but whatever it is causes Sarah to tell Abraham to send Ishmael and Hagar away, denying Ishmael a share of Abraham's inheritance. Reluctant, Abraham turns to God for guidance, and God tells him to listen to Sarah and to do as Sarah says. Abraham sends Hagar and Ishmael away with the understanding that Ishmael's future will be safeguarded, but God's promise will be fulfilled through Isaac.

Sarah lives until the age of 127 and is the only woman in scripture whose age at death is given. There are references to Abraham's mourning and weeping (Genesis 23:2) and in Genesis 24 to her son Isaac's bringing his wife-to-be Rebekah into his mother's tent, where Rebekah comforts Isaac as he grieves for his mother.

Sarah embodies the Advent message of hope: there is always hope for new life even in circumstances of apparent barrenness. She teaches us to laugh, even to laugh in response to God's message of hope for us, and to laugh with one another in joy. Is anything too wonderful for God?

Symbols: images of laughter, a map of Sarai/Sarah and Abram/Abraham's travels, living plants in a dessert, a pregnant woman, a tent in the wilderness, artist's rendering of Sarah

Questions for Reflection:

How does Sarah demonstrate her faithfulness to God and God to her?

Have you received news so unexpected that it seemed impossible but that turned out to be true? What was your response?

How is the partnership between God and Sarah similar to that of God and Eve?

What do you think about Sarai's relationships with the Pharaoh of Egypt and King Abimelech? What do we learn about Sarai/Sarah in these situations? About Abram/Abraham?

Why is Hagar an essential part of this story? What is God's role in the outcome?

In what ways is Sarah a woman of Advent?

REBEKAH

Scriptural References: Genesis 24-29, 35, 49

Her brother and her mother said, "Let the girl remain with us for a while, at least ten days; after that she may go." But he said to them, "Do not delay me, since the Lord has made my journey successful; let me go that I may go to my master." They said, "We will call the girl, and ask her." And they called Rebekah, and said to her, "Will you go with this man?" She said, "I will." "So they sent away their sister Rebekah and her nurse along with Abraham's servant and his men. And they blessed Rebekah and said to her, "May you, our sister, become thousands of myriads; may your offspring gain possession of the gates of their foes." Then Rebekah and her maids rose up, mounted the camels, and followed the man; thus the servant took Rebekah, and went on his way.

Now Isaac had come from Beerlahairoi, and was settled in the Negeb. Isaac went out in the evening to walk in the field; and looking up, he saw camels coming. And Rebekah looked up, and when she saw Isaac, she slipped quickly from the camel, and said to the servant, "Who is the man over there, walking in the field to meet us?" The servant said, "It is my master." So she took her veil and covered herself. And the servant told Isaac all the things that he had done. Then Isaac brought her into his mother Sarah's tent. He took Rebekah, and she became his wife; and he loved her. So Isaac was comforted after his mother's death. (Genesis 24:55-67)

Think men are running this show? Meet Rebekah, matriarch of the generation following Sarah. The family lineage from Abraham to Isaac to Jacob is clear, but the succession catalyst is Rebekah. Her mode is action: she runs, draws water, welcomes and nourishes, creates a sizzling love-at-first sight scene with Isaac, and eventually controls the family's destiny. When her son, Jacob, meets his future wife Rachel, Jacob tells Rachel not that he is the son of Isaac, but the son of Rebekah.

Rebecca's story appears principally in Chapters 24-27 of Genesis. She enters the picture in an arranged marriage with Isaac. Early on, we learn about Rebekah's character through her interactions with Abraham's representative who has come to Mesopotamia to find a wife for Isaac. The opening scene takes place at a well as Rebekah comes out carrying a water jug. She quickly gives water to the stranger, welcoming him, providing water for his camels, and offering a place in her father's house for the night. The account of Rebekah at the well reveals not only her beauty, but her virtues in hospitality, befriending a stranger and caring for his animals. From those moments, Rebekah is the certain choice for Isaac's future wife in the eyes of Abraham's servant, an answer to his own prayer.

Rebekah has some say in the matter of marital negotiations, as her family asks if she will go with the man. She agrees to accompany the representative back to meet her potential fiancé, Isaac. Upon arrival, Rebekah enters Isaac's home, which is his mother Sarah's tent, and she comforts Isaac in his grief over the death of his mother.

For many years, Rebekah is barren. Isaac prays for his wife, and she finally conceives. But the pregnancy is torturous. The babies struggle in Rebekah's womb, and she asks God why she has to live through something so difficult. God responds,

"Two nations are in your womb, and two peoples born of you shall be divided; the one shall be stronger than the other, the elder shall serve the younger" (Genesis 25:23). Rebekah gives birth to twin sons, Esau the elder and Jacob the younger. Esau grows up to be a skilled hunter, a 'man of the field,' and Jacob a 'quiet man,' living in tents. Because he is fond of game, Isaac favors Esau, but Rebekah favors Jacob.

When there is famine in the land, Rebekah and Isaac, like Sarah and Abraham before them, travel to Gerar, land of King Abimelech; a busy kingdom. Again, the episode is similar to Sarah's experience. Although Isaac passes Rebekah off as his sister so she can be with Abimelech, in this version Rebekah's marital fidelity to Isaac is never compromised, and Rebekah is returned to Isaac.

In the dramatic family scene recounted in Genesis 27, Rebekah deceives Isaac, who is nearly blind. As a result of the confusion, Isaac gives his blessing to Jacob rather than to elder son, Esau. When Esau recognizes his loss, he asks his father for a blessing also, but Isaac refuses, saying, "By your sword you shall live, and you shall serve your brother" (Genesis 27:40).

Feeling hatred toward Jacob, Esau plans to kill him. But Rebekah intervenes, sending Jacob to safety with her brother Laban in Haran until Esau's "anger against him turns away....Why should I lose you both in one day?" (Genesis 27:44).

When Jacob eventually meets his future bride, Rachel, he kisses her, weeps aloud, and tells her that he is Rebekah's son. It is through Rebekah's resourcefulness (or deft manipulation) that Jacob secures the position as heir to Isaac's ancestral lineage rather than Esau as the first-born son, fulfilling what God has told Rebekah in response to her question about the difficult pregnancy: the elder shall serve the younger.

Symbols: Water jar, well, camel, tent, woman holding twins, artist's rendering of Rebekah.

Questions for Reflection:

How does the story of Rebekah advance Sarah's story as a female leader?

What do we learn about Rebekah's life that is consistent with her initial interaction with Isaac's representative? What qualities are admirable?

Why is the story of Rebekah and Isaac sometimes called the first biblical 'love story'?

Why does Rebekah deceive Isaac, and how do you assess her role in the deception?

Have you ever been in a position requiring fierce protection of a loved one and if so, what was your response?

How is Rebekah a woman of Advent?

TAMAR

Scriptural References, Genesis 38, Matthew 1:2-3

She saw that Shelah was grown up, yet she had not been given to him in marriage. When Judah saw her, he thought her to be a prostitute, for she had covered her face. He went over to her at the road side and said, "Come, let me come in to you," for he did not know that she was his daughter-in-law. She said, "What will you give me, that you may come into me?" He answered, "I will send you a kid from the flock." And she said, "Only if you give me a pledge, until you send it." He said, "What pledge shall I give you?" She replied, "Your signet and your cord, and the staff that is in your hand." So he gave them to her, and went in to her, and she conceived by him. Then she got up and went away, and taking off her veil she put on the garments of her widowhood.

> When Judah sent the kid by his friend the Adullamite, to recover the pledge from the woman, he could not find her. He asked the townspeople, "Where is the temple prostitute who was at Enaim by the wayside?" But they said, "No prostitute has been here." So he returned to Judah, and said, "I have not found her; moreover the townspeople said, 'No prostitute has been here.'" Judah replied, "Let her keep the things as her own, otherwise we will be laughed at; you see, I sent this kid, and you could not find her." (Genesis 38:14-23)

The Gospel of Matthew lists Tamar as the first woman in the genealogy of Jesus: "Abraham was the father of Isaac, and Isaac the father of Jacob, and Jacob the father of Judah and his brothers, and Judah the father of Perez and Zerah by Tamar" (Matthew 1:2-3).

Given her place in the lineage of Jesus, it seems that her story would be one of the most important we would read and hear from scripture. But we don't, at least not in church. Chapter 38, the source of Tamar's narrative in Genesis, appears neither in the Revised Common Lectionary for Sunday readings or the Daily Office Lectionary. Why? It's a messy story. The people of God misbehave on multiple levels, so rife with sex and violence that the story could top the bestseller list in today's culture.

The laws of God, by which Israel lives, are clearly stated in the Book of Deuteronomy. One of these statutes (Deuteronomy 25:5-6) addresses the appropriate actions for a widow following the death of her husband. When an Israelite man dies and has no son, the wife of the deceased man is not permitted to marry outside the family. Instead, the dead husband's brother is to marry her and perform the duty of a husband. Her firstborn shall have the name of her deceased husband so that his name will not be blotted out of Israel.

Tamar takes extraordinary steps to follow this law in order to engender children according to its rule.

The story begins with her eventual father-in-law, Judah, who is the fourth son of Jacob and Leah as well as the founder of one of the twelve tribes of Israel. Judah marries the daughter of Shua, who bears three sons–Er, Onan, and Shelah. Judah takes Tamar as a wife for Er, but Er's wickedness in the sight of God results in his death. Following the law, Judah instructs Onan to go to Tamar and perform the brother-in-law *duty* in order to produce an offspring for his brother. But Onan doesn't want to do that since the child wouldn't be his, so he spills his semen on the ground. Such a loss to humanity.

God doesn't like that action either and puts Onan to death, leaving Judah with only one other option, to have Tamar remain in his house as a widow until Shelah matures. When Shelah grows up, however, he isn't given to Tamar in marriage as promised. If she is to have an offspring, Tamar recognizes that she needs to develop her own plan.

This brings us back to Judah. After his own wife dies and he finishes the period of grieving, he decides to go to Timnah to shear his sheep. When Tamar hears of this journey, she takes off her own widow's garments, puts on a veil, wraps herself up, and sits at the entrance to Enaim on the road to Timnah. When Judah sees her, he thinks she's a prostitute and asks her to let him come to her. Thinking ahead, she agrees on the condition that he give her a pledge to secure eventual payment of a kid from his flock. What pledge? "Your signet ring and your cord, and the staff that is in your hand" (Genesis 38:18). Judah gives them to Tamar in pledge, goes to her, and she conceives by him.

When Judah subsequently sends a friend back to give payment and recover the pledge, the friend cannot find the prostitute. According to the townspeople, there is no prostitute (Genesis 38:21). So Judah decides that the prostitute can just keep his stuff; otherwise, he'll be laughed at.

Three months later, Judah learns that Tamar "is pregnant as a result of whoredom" (Genesis 38:24). He orders her brought out to be burned. She's to be burned because of *his* actions. Tamar sends word that the owner of signet ring, cord, and shepherd's staff is the man who has gotten her pregnant. Judah recognizes these items as his own. Finally, he acknowledges, "She is more in the right than I, since I did not give her to my son Shelah" (Genesis 38:26). And Judah does not lie with her again. Tamar gives birth to twins, Perez and Zerah, of the Jesus lineage. Abraham is the father of Isaac, Jacob is the father of Judah, and Judah is the father of Perez and Zerah by Tamar. Without Tamar, without her ingenuity and perseverance, according to the Matthew's genealogy, there would be no Jesus.

Symbols: Shepherd's staff, kid goat, twins, artist's rendering of Tamar

Questions for Reflection:

Why does Tamar have a key role in Jesus' genealogy?

Why is this story included in the biblical narrative?

What are Tamar's unique contributions to the biblical narrative?

What do you think about Tamar's relationship to God? Her relationship to Judah? About Judah's actions?

Why don't churches include this story in Sunday readings? Would this story be interesting to hear and discuss in a worship setting?

What does Tamar uniquely offer for the Advent themes hope and expectation?

MIRIAM

*Scriptural References: Exodus 2, 15,
Numbers 12, 20:1, 26:59
Deuteronomy 24:9; 1 Chronicles 6:3, Micah 6:4*

Now a man from the house of Levi went and married a Levite woman. The woman conceived and bore a son; and when she saw that he was a fine baby, she hid him three months. When she could hide him no longer she got a papyrus basket for him, and plastered it with bitumen and pitch; she put the child in it and placed it among the reeds on the bank of the river. His sister stood at a distance, to see what would happen to him....

Then the prophet Miriam, Aaron's sister, took a tambourine in her hand; and all the women went out after her with tambourines and with dancing. And Miriam sang to them....

So Miriam was shut out of the camp for seven days; and the people did not set out on the march until Miriam had been brought in again (Exodus 2:1-4; 15:20-21; Numbers 12:15).

The sister of Moses appears in the second chapter of Exodus, and she is identified as Miriam by genealogies (Numbers 26:59, 1 Chronicles 6:3) that list Moses, Aaron, and Miriam as the only children of Amram. The hereditary line is from Abraham to Isaac to Jacob to Levi to Kohath to Amram.

To save Moses from the Egyptian Pharaoh's edict to kill all male Hebrew children, Moses' mother places him in a basket on the bank of the Nile River, and Miriam watches to see what will happen to him. Pharaoh's daughter comes to bathe, sees the basket among the reeds, sends her maid to retrieve it, and they recognize a Hebrew child.

After watching these developments unfold, Miriam approaches and offers to get a nurse for the baby from the Hebrew women. Pharaoh's daughter agrees in a gutsy move of her own to defy her father, and Miriam brings the baby back to their own mother to raise him. When the child grows up, Pharaoh's daughter takes him for her own son and names him Moses.

Several events later–a burning bush, Israel's deliverance, ten plagues, the Israeli exodus, pillars of cloud and fire, the parting of the Red Sea, the drowning of Egyptian pursuers–Miriam appears once again in Exodus 15. She leads a victory celebration among all the women, singing and dancing and playing tambourines.

Miriam is the first woman in scripture to have the title of prophet, and the Song of Miriam (Exodus 15:20-21) is an important part of female traditions in scripture that include other songs, such as those of Deborah and Hannah. We read more about Miriam in later scripture when she speaks against Moses because of the woman he marries (Numbers 12:1-6). With her brother Aaron, Miriam challenges the authority of Moses' approach to leadership as she understands leadership to reflect voices other than that solely of Moses. "Has the Lord spoken only through Moses? Has he not spoken through us also?" (Numbers 12:2).

God reprimands both Miriam and Aaron, but punishes only Miriam, leaving her leprous, as white as snow. Aaron speaks up for her, and Moses cries out to God to heal her. But God's answer is to shut her out of camp for seven days of purification before being allowed to return. She doesn't speak again in scripture, either in voice or action, but the people speak for her. When Miriam is excluded from camp, they refuse to march until she has returned to them (Numbers 12:15).

Miriam is known for saving Moses as a baby, for her role as a female prophet, for leading the celebration of the Red Sea victory, and more broadly for her power and partnership with Aaron and Moses in leading early Israel in the exodus and subsequent wanderings. The people remain loyal to Miriam in spite of the conflict with God. Nature, too, honors Miriam: at her death, the waters of Meribah dry up, and Moses brings water from the rock (Numbers 20:1-2,11). She is recognized in Micah as an equal to Moses and Aaron (Micah 6:4).

We continue to hear echoes of Miriam through song, dance, and instruments in the psalms. "The singers in front, the musicians last, between them girls playing tambourines" (68:25); "Raise a song, sound the tambourine, the sweet lyre with the harp" (81:2); "Praise God with tambourine and dance" (150:4).

Symbols: tambourine, women dancing, woman with baby in a basket, woman leading women in song and dance, icon of Miriam

Questions for Reflection:

What do we learn about Miriam from her initial appearance at the Nile River?

How does Miriam lead?

What is Miriam's relationship to God? To her brothers? To her people?

What does Miriam protest, in a broader sense than Moses alone speaking?

Why does God treat Miriam differently from Aaron? What is the response by those in camp?

What does Miriam bring uniquely to our own worship experience?

How does Miriam embody the spirit of Advent?

RAHAB

Scriptural References: Joshua 2, 6, Matthew 1:5, Hebrews 11:31, James 2:25

Then Joshua son of Nun sent two men secretly from Shittim as spies, saying, "Go, view the land, especially Jericho." So they went, and entered the house of a prostitute whose name was Rahab, and spent the night there. The king of Jericho was told, "Some Israelites have come here tonight to search out the land." Then the king of Jericho sent orders to Rahab, "Bring out the men who have come to you, who entered your house, for they have come only to search out the land." But the woman took the two men and hid them. Then she said, "True, the men came to me, but I did not know where they came from. And when it was time to close the gate at dark, the men went out. Where the men went I do not know. Pursue them quickly, for you can overtake them. She had, however, brought them up to the roof and hidden them with the stalks of flax that she had laid out on the roof. So the men pursued them on the way to the Jordan as far as the fords. As soon as the pursuers had gone out, the gate was shut.

Before they went to sleep, she came up to them on the roof and said to the men: "I know that the Lord has given you the land, and that dread of you has fallen on us, and that all the inhabitants of the land melt in fear before you. For we have heard how the Lord dried up the water of the Red Sea before when you came out of Egypt, and what you did to the two kings of the Amorites that were beyond the Jordan, to Sihon and Og, whom you utterly destroyed. As soon as we heard it, our hearts melted, and there was no courage left in any of us because of you. The Lord your God is indeed God in heaven above and on earth below. Now then, since I have dealt kindly with you, swear to me by the Lord that you in turn will deal kindly with my family. Give me a sign of good faith that you will spare my father and mother, my brothers and sisters, and all who belong to them, and deliver our lives from death." The men said to her, "Our life for yours! If you do not tell this business of ours, then we will deal kindly and faithfully with you when the Lord gives us the land." Then she let them down by a rope through the window, for her house was on the outer side of the city wall and she resided within the wall itself (Joshua 2:1-15).

Joshua sends two spies to Jericho in preparation for entry into the Promised Land, beginning with the battle for Jericho. Needing a place to spend the night, they go to the house of the prostitute, Rahab. When the King of Jericho is made aware of their presence, he has word sent to Rahab to bring them out. Instead, she says she doesn't know where they have gone and encourages the king's men to pursue them.

Meanwhile, Rahab hides the spies on the roof and talks to them about her vision and understanding of God's promise of land for Israel. She quotes from history about the drying up of the Red Sea and previous battle victories. If they will spare her family in the attack of Jericho, she will help them escape, an offer to which the men reply, "Our life for yours!" (Joshua 2:14). They make a commitment to deal kindly with her and her family when God gives them the land. Since Rahab's house is located on the outer side of the city wall, she lets them down with a rope, and they escape.

The story continues with Rahab telling the men to go into the hill country and hide for three days, then go back to make their report to Joshua. The men instruct Rahab to tie a crimson cord in the window through which they escaped, to gather all her family into the house, and not to tell anyone of their plans. She sends them away and ties the cord in the window. They return to Joshua after the three days of hiding and tell Joshua all that has happened.

When Joshua succeeds in the destruction of Jericho, Rahab and her family escape capture by waiting in the house marked with the crimson cord. They are brought out of the city to live in Israel. "But Rahab the prostitute, with her family and all who belonged to her, Joshua spared. Her family has lived in Israel ever since. For she hid the messengers whom Joshua sent to spy out of Jericho" (Joshua 6:25).

Rahab's historical role is cited twice in the New Testament: in the Letter to the Hebrews: "By faith, the walls of Jericho fell after they had been encircled for seven days. By faith Rahab the prostitute did not perish with those who were disobedient, because she had received the spies in peace" (Hebrews 11:30-31) as well as in the Letter of James. Rahab is listed in Matthew's lineage of Jesus as the wife of Salmon, father of Boaz (Matthew 5:5), which would mean (if it is the same Rahab) that she eventually married into one of the leading families of Israel.

It is in large measure thanks to Rahab that, in the words of the African-American spiritual, "Joshua fights the battle of Jericho, and the walls come a-tumbling down." Rahab enters biblical narrative like the slave who composed the hymn, marginalized; Rahab is marginalized as a woman and a prostitute. Through her compassion, quick-thinking, faith, and vision, she becomes a courageous savior and mother of Israel.

Symbols: Crimson cord, artist's rendering of Rahab

Questions for Reflection:

Why is the role of savior and visionary specifically given to Rahab by the biblical writers?

How and why does Rahab come up with her plan?

What is Rahab's vision?

What is Rahab's relationship with God? With her family? With the men in the story?

How and why was the battle of Jericho won?

Have you been in situations where the 'marginalized' become leaders?

How does Rahab embody the spirit of Advent?

DEBORAH

Scriptural References: Judges 4, 5

At that time Deborah, a prophetess, wife of Lappidoth, was judging Israel. She used to sit under the palm of Deborah between Ramah and Bethel in the hill country of Ephraim; and the Israelites came up to her for judgment. She sent and summoned Barak son of Abinoam from Kedesh in Naphtali, and said to him, "The Lord, the God of Israel, commands you, 'Go take position at Mount Tabor, bringing ten thousand from the tribe of Naphtali and the tribe of Zebulun. I will draw out Sisera, the general of Jabin's army, to meet you by the Wadi Kishon with his chariots and troops; and I will give him into your hand.'" Barak said to her, "If you will go with me, I will go; but if you will not go with me, I will not go." And she said, "I will surely go with you; nevertheless, the road on which you are going will not lead to your glory, for the Lord will sell Sisera into the hand of a wom-

an." Then Deborah got up and went with Barak to Kedesh. Barak summoned Zebulun and Naphtali to Kedesh; and ten thousand warriors went up behind him; and Deborah went up with him (Judges 4:4-10).

The Israelites make another mess and are once again in trouble with God, back in the clutches of the King Jabin of Canaan. They cry to God for help, for deliverance from the Canaanites who have nine hundred chariots of iron in their arsenal and have cruelly oppressed them for twenty years.

As the story begins, they come to Deborah to request guidance. A powerful combination, Deborah is both female judge and prophet. In a temporarily bucolic opening scene, she sits in the hill country under the palm of Deborah rendering judgments.

With directions from God, Deborah devises a plan to save Israel. She summons Barak, her battle general, relaying to him the instructions from God to take ten thousand men up to Mount Tabor and begin the siege. Barak says to her that he will go only if she will go with him. Deborah agrees to go with him into battle.

Imagine such a strategy, the leader who sends the troops into battle being willing to go with them. We might never have war. The other highly unusual caveat, set by Deborah, is guts but no glory. Barak is to accrue no accolades for his efforts.

The Israelites, led by Barak, succeed in battle, destroying all of the Canaanite enemies except the major leader, Sisera. Sisera flees the scene and seeks refuge with a woman named Jael. In a surprising twist, Jael steps up on behalf of the Israelites and kills Sisera, driving a tent peg into his temple with a hammer and sealing the deal for the Israeli army.

Chapter 5 of Judges, "The Song of Deborah," offers poetic lyrics to describe the teamwork in battle. "Awake, awake, Deborah! Awake, awake, utter a song! Arise, Barak, lead away your captives, O son of Abinoam. Then down marched the remnant of the noble; the people of the Lord marched down for him against the mighty" (Judges 5:12-13). She credits the providential help they received along the battle way: "The stars fought from heaven, from their courses they fought against Sisera. The torrent Kishon swept them away, the onrushing torrent, the torrent Kishon. March on, my soul, with might!" (Judges 5:20-21). Appropriately, she honors Jael, who is the key to ultimate victory, "Most blessed of women be Jael" (Judges 5:24).

As the only biblical character who is both a prophet and a judge, Deborah recognizes the enormous challenges that confront her people and adds a unique dimension to the role God has chosen for her in the ongoing efforts to secure the Promised Land. A female military leader, she accompanies the troops into battle and honors all of her colleagues for their work in the name of God. Her unprecedented contributions as a biblical heroine are recognized through the duel telling and celebration of her story, in prose (Judges 4) and in song (Judges 5). And the land had rest for forty years.

Symbols: Scales of justice, palm tree, artist's rendering of Deborah

Questions for Reflection:

Why did God choose Deborah for this story? Why is a female the only biblical character who is both judge and prophet?

How does Deborah respond?

What is unique about the relationship Deborah has with Barak?

What do we learn about Deborah's relationship with God through her actions?

How do you assess Jael's contributions?

What do you think it would be like to share a foxhole with Deborah?

How does Deborah embody the spirit of Advent?

RUTH

Scriptural References: Ruth 1-4

So she said, "See, your sister-in-law has gone back to her people and to her gods; return after your sister-in-law." But Ruth said, "Do not press me to leave you or to turn back from following you! Where you go, I will go; where you lodge I will lodge; your people shall be my people, and your God my God. Where you die, I will die—there will I be buried. May the Lord do thus and so to me, and more as well, if even death parts me from you!" When Naomi saw that she was determined to go with her, she said no more to her. So the two of them went on until they came to Bethlehem. When they came to Bethlehem, the whole town was stirred because of them; and the women said, Is this Naomi?..."

So Naomi returned together with Ruth the Moabite, her daughter-in-law, who came back with her from the coun-

try of Moab. They came to Bethlehem at the beginning of the barley harvest. Now Naomi had a kinsman on her husband's side, a prominent rich man of the family of Elimelech, whose name was Boaz. And Ruth the Moabite said to Naomi, "Let me go to the field and glean among the ears of grain, behind someone in whose sight I may find favor." She said to her, "Go, my daughter." (Ruth 1:15-19, 22, 2:1-2)

Ruth has an entire four-chapter book of the Old Testament devoted to her life. Her story begins in Moab with marriage to a Judean immigrant. He dies after ten years, leaving Ruth as a childless widow. Instead of remaining in her home country, Ruth chooses to leave her own family, religion, and land in order to accompany her mother-in-law, Naomi, to Judah, even though Naomi discourages this decision.

In announcing her plan, Ruth pledges her unequivocal faithfulness. "Where you go, I will go; where you lodge, I will lodge; your people shall be my people, and your God my God. Where you die, I will die—there will I be buried. May the Lord do thus and so to me, and more as well, if even death parts me from you!" (Ruth 1:16-17). Committing her way to an older woman is a radical choice for Ruth in a culture where life depends on men.

Naomi's response to this loyalty and faithfulness? When the women come into Bethlehem, she doesn't acknowledge Ruth's presence, saying she (Naomi) went away full and has returned empty. But Ruth stays.

Ruth resolves to go out and find food; this choice comes with Naomi's blessing. As it happens, she comes into the field of grain belonging to Boaz, a relative of Naomi on her husband's side. Loyal patriarch that he is, Boaz asks to whom Ruth belongs. When he learns that she came with Naomi, he allows Ruth to glean in his field. Boaz recognizes Ruth's uniqueness as one who has left her family and homeland to live among people she does not know, and he invokes a blessing from God: "May God reward you for your deeds and may you have full reward from the God of Israel" (Ruth 2:12). This pleases Naomi who encourages her to go out with the young women in Boaz's field.

The action gets steamy when Naomi, to ensure Ruth's future safety and position, instructs her to make herself *available* to Boaz by going to him on the threshing room floor after the harvest celebration. Ruth does as Naomi says, coming stealthily after Boaz has eaten, drunk, and is *in a contented mood*. She uncovers his feet and lies down. He is startled, turns over and asks who she is. Ruth tells him who she is, and instead of a seduction, the scene becomes one of blessing: Boaz recognizing Ruth's loyalty. When she reports all to her mother-in-law, bringing six measures of barley for her because Boaz knew not to send her home empty-handed, Naomi tells Ruth the 'matter' will be settled that day.

Ruth becomes the subject of community gossip at the city gate where Boaz presents the case of Ruth for whom an unnamed man has first marital rights. When the 'man' finds out his 'rights' include the necessity of purchasing land from Naomi in order to marry Ruth, he backs out, opening the door for Boaz the redeemer, which takes place with the exchange of a sandal.

Boaz explains he is marrying Ruth, the wife of the Moabite Mahlon, to maintain the dead man's inheritance. The city elders compare Ruth with ancestral mothers, seeing Ruth as the fulfillment of traditional values and continuing the male lineage. "May the Lord make the woman who is coming into your house like Rachel and Leah, who together built up the house of Israel" (Ruth 4:11).

Boaz acquires the relevant land, Ruth and Boaz marry, and she bears a son. Ruth's story ends with Naomi taking the child, laying him to her bosom, and becoming his nurse. The women in the village, saying the son has been born to Naomi, name him Obed, father of Jesse, father of David. Whatever the village women claim, Ruth is the great-grandmother of David and continues the lineage.

In the Gospel of Matthew, the genealogy is listed as "…Salmon the father of Boaz by Rahab, and Boaz the father of Obed by Ruth, and Obed the father of Jesse, and Jesse the father of King David" (Matthew 1:4-6), reflecting much effort and ingenuity to get these boys born.

Symbols: barley, a young and older woman traveling, a woman gleaning in a field of grain, artist's rendering of Ruth

Questions for Reflection:

What do you think Ruth's pledge reveals about her decision to leave her ancestral home and accompany Naomi? Why is hers an oft-quoted statement?

Why does Naomi ignore Ruth when they arrive in Bethlehem?

What is Ruth's response to Naomi?

What do you think of Boaz's role in this story? Who's in charge here, Ruth or Boaz? Or Naomi?

Why does Ruth accommodate the behavior of those around her?

How does Ruth confront/honor patriarchy?

In what ways does Ruth reflect the Advent themes of hope and expectation?

ESTHER

Scriptural References: Esther 1-10

On the third day Esther put on her royal robes and stood in the inner court of the king's palace, opposite the king's hall. The king was sitting on his royal throne inside the palace opposite the entrance to the palace. As soon as the king saw Queen Esther standing in the court, she won his favor and he held out to her the golden scepter that was in his hand. Then Esther approached and touched the top of the scepter. The king said to her, "What is it, Queen Esther? What is your request? It shall be given you, even to the half of my kingdom…. Then Esther answered, "If I have won your favor, O king, and if it pleases the king, let my life be given me—that is my petition—and the lives of my people—that is my request." (Esther 5:1-3, 7:3-4)

Like Ruth, Esther's contributions to the biblical history are narrated in a separate book of the Old Testament. Esther is a young, Jewish woman living with her exiled people in Persia, and her story begins in the harem of King Ahasuerus, where she is one of the young virgins.

Queen Vashti has failed to obey her husband the king, not *coming to him* when he commands her to do so. Bad Queen? Enraged, the king issues a proclamation that women are supposed to obey their husbands, high and low alike. Once his anger abates, he decides to have beautiful young virgins brought in for review. He'll find one who pleases him.

Enter Esther, cousin of Mordecai. Esther is brought in and put into custody of Hegai, the king's chief eunuch, who has charge of the harem. She is provided with cosmetic treatments and food. Mordecai has told her not to reveal that she is Jewish, and he monitors her progress as he walks around the court each day.

Esther is admired by all who see her. When Esther's turn comes to spend the night with the king, he loves her more than all the other virgins. She wins his favor and devotion, and he makes her queen instead of Vashti, giving a celebratory "Esther's Banquet" to officials and ministers, and granting a holiday to the provinces.

As she begins her reign, Queen Esther's cousin Mordecai uncovers a plot to assassinate the king. Mordecai shares this intelligence with Esther, who tells the king in the name of Mordecai. The secretive affair is investigated and confirmed. Mordecai, however, soon gets into a power struggle and refuses to bow before Haman, head of the king's officials. Haman vows to slaughter Mordecai and his entire people, securing the king's permission to act.

A date is set for the slaughter, the thirteenth day of Adar. When Mordecai learns of this plot, he gets word to Esther, but it is at risk of death for her to approach the king. "All the king's servants and the people of the king's provinces know that if any man or woman goes to the king inside the inner court without being called, there is but one law—all alike are to be put to death" (Esther 4:12).

Queen Esther vows to find a way to save her people. She instructs Mordecai to gather all the Jews and hold a fast for three days. She and her maids will fast also. After that, she will go to the king, in spite of going against the law, and "if I perish, I perish" (Esther 4:16). On the third day, she stands in the inner court. As soon as the king sees Esther, he holds out to her the golden scepter in his hand. Esther slyly issues her request, which is for the king to throw a banquet, to be attended by Haman. During that feast, Esther makes a request for yet another dinner party.

Haman becomes suspicious and has gallows built for Mordecai. It is at the second party that Esther reveals her true objective and herself as a Jew, "let my life be given me—that is my petition—and the lives of my people—that is my request" (Esther 7:3).

After Esther exposes Haman's plot to destroy her people, King Ahasuerus has him executed on the gallows he built for Mordecai. The Jews are given permission to defend themselves, and they gain relief from their enemies.

Not unlike some of the other Advent women, sex and sexual favors are an important part of Esther's story and ascension to power. But she shows that by effort and ingenuity, her people can survive and prosper. Initially powerless in the Persian Empire, the Jews living in Persia are given hope and encouragement by Esther.

The book of Esther ends with Mordecai elevated to the position as top official, next in rank to King Ahasuerus, and a concentration of power in the hands of Queen Esther. The command of Queen Esther fixes practices of Purim, recorded in writing, and letters are sent wishing peace and security to all the Jews throughout the nation.

Queen Vashti is notable in the story as a woman who refuses to obey a male, a male in the highest position of power; in essence, she succeeds in her objective, which is *not to be with* King Ahasuerus.

Although God is never mentioned in Esther's story, there are religious practices, such as the three days of fasting, evidencing God's presence and alliance with Esther in saving her people, as well as Esther's demonstrating her faith in God. The Jewish celebration of Purim in the spring occurs on the thirteenth day of Adar to celebrate the time when the Jewish people living in Persia were saved from extermination.

Symbols: Scepter, Jewish star, artist's rendering of Esther

Questions for Reflection:

Why does Esther have her own book in the Old Testament?

Why does the Old Testament include a book in which God is not mentioned?

How do you assess Queen Vashti's role in the story? Mordecai's? King Ahasuerus?

What do you think about Esther's beginnings as a virgin in the King's harem?

What are the risks taken by Esther, and why is she a biblical heroine?

What is Esther's relationship to God?

How does Esther embody the spirit of Advent?

ELIZABETH

Scriptural References: Luke 1:5-66

In the days of King Herod of Judea, there was a priest named Zechariah, who belonged to the priestly order of Abijah. His wife was a descendant of Aaron, and her name was Elizabeth. Both of them were righteous before God, living blamelessly according to all the commandments and regulations of the Lord. But they had no children because Elizabeth was barren, and both were getting on in years....

But the angel said to him, "Do not be afraid, Zechariah, for your prayer has been heard. Your wife Elizabeth will bear you a son, and you will name him John. You will have joy and gladness, and many will rejoice at his birth, for he will be great in the sight of the Lord. He must never drink wine or strong drink; even before his birth, he will be filled with the Holy Spirit...."

After those days his wife Elizabeth conceived, and for five months she remained in seclusion. She said, "This is what the Lord has done for me when he looked favorably on me and took away the disgrace I have endured among my people...."

In those days Mary set out and went with haste to a Judean town in the hill country, where she entered the house of Zechariah and greeted Elizabeth. When Elizabeth heard Mary's greeting, the child leaped in her womb. And Elizabeth was filled with the Holy Spirit and exclaimed with a loud cry, "Blessed are you among women, and blessed is the fruit of your womb. And why has this happened to me, that the mother of my Lord comes to me? For as soon as I heard the sound of your greeting, the child in my womb leaped for joy. And blessed is she who believed that there would be a fulfillment of what was spoken to her by the Lord...."

And Mary remained with her about three months and then returned to her home....

Now the time came for Elizabeth to give birth, and she bore a son. Her neighbors and relatives heard that the Lord had shown his great mercy to her, and they rejoiced with her.

On the eighth day they came to circumcise the child, and they were going to name him Zechariah after his father. But his mother said, "No; he is to be called John." They said to her, "None of your relatives has this name." Then they began motioning to his father to find out what name he want-

ed to give him. He asked for a writing tablet and wrote, "His name is John." And all of them were amazed. (Luke 1:5-7; 13-15; 24-25; 39-45; 56-63)

Elizabeth quietly makes her way into the Advent story, beginning in much the same way as some of her predecessors: barren. Her story in the first chapter of Luke intertwines with those of Mary and Zechariah, but she has much to offer as a singular figure.

While serving as a temple priest, Elizabeth's husband Zechariah has an angel encounter during which he hears that Elizabeth will bear a son who will be named John, bringing joy and gladness. Even before this child's birth, he will be filled with the Holy Spirit, quite a bundle for Elizabeth to nurture in her womb.

As promised, Elizabeth conceives, and she remains in seclusion for five months, relieved that she has been released from the cultural 'disgrace' of not bearing a child. In the sixth month of Elizabeth's pregnancy, her cousin Mary is visited by God's angel, Gabriel with the prophecy of Mary's own pregnancy. The angel reminds Mary of another family 'miracle': that her cousin Elizabeth has conceived in her old age.

Hastily, Mary comes to visit Elizabeth in the hill country and greets her. In response to this greeting, Elizabeth's child leaps in her womb. A strong kicker. The exchange between the women fills Elizabeth with the Holy Spirit. In gratitude for the fulfillment of God's promises, Elizabeth offers a profound blessing, a blessing of Mary's womb and the fruit of her womb. Mary responds with her own song of praise to God and remains with Elizabeth for three months before returning home.

When the time comes for Elizabeth's labor and delivery, she gives birth to a son, and neighbors and relatives rejoice with her. Eight days following the birth, the extended family comes together for the circumcision and naming of the child. The relatives' plan is to name him Zechariah, after his father. But Elizabeth announces that his name is John, which leads to protest by the assembly because no other relative has this name.

Zechariah, who had been struck dumb because he did not believe God's promise of Elizabeth's pregnancy, enters the scene and confirms, by writing on a tablet, what Elizabeth has said, that their son's name is John. All are amazed as Zechariah's tongue is freed and he is able to speak again.

Elizabeth contributes in unique ways to the spiritual narrative of Jesus' eventual birth and ministry. First, the response to the angel's prophecy to Zechariah of Elizabeth's pregnancy is met differently by the couple: Elizabeth believes it, sustained by faith and hope, while Zechariah so questions this news that he loses the ability to speak. Elizabeth demonstrates the value and meaning of *sanctuary* as she shelters her cousin Mary in an out-of-wedlock pregnancy for three months, providing support and blessing for her. Both women reflect the unwavering faith that their wombs are filled with God's promise. Standing up to the extended family members who attempt to control the naming of her son, Elizabeth declares that his name is John, as foretold in the angel's prophecy to Zechariah. Elizabeth's son John grows into the man who prepares the way for Jesus' ministry.

Symbols: Angel, home as sanctuary, pregnant women, tablet, artist's rendering of Elizabeth

Questions for Reflection:

What is unique about Elizabeth's story relative to other women of Advent who are barren?

Why do you think there is a difference in reactions to the angel's prophecy to Zechariah?

How is a model of sanctuary shown in the story? Why is that important to them and to us?

What do we learn about Elizabeth's relationship to Zechariah? To her culture? To Mary?

In what ways is Elizabeth a woman of Advent?

MARY

Scriptural References: Matthew 1:12-25, 2:1-21; 12:46-50; 13:55; Mark 3:31-35; 6:3; Luke 1:26-56; 2:1-51; 8:19-21; John 2:1-12; 19:25-27; Acts 1:14

Now the birth of Jesus the Messiah took place in this way. When his mother Mary had been engaged to Joseph, but before they lived together, she was found to be with child from the Holy Spirit. Her husband Joseph, being a righteous man and unwilling to expose her to public disgrace, planned to dismiss her quietly. But just when he had resolved to do this, an angel of the Lord appeared to him in a dream and said, "Joseph, son of David, do not be afraid to take Mary as your wife, for the child conceived in her is from the Holy Spirit. She will bear a son, and you are to name him Jesus for he will save his people from their sins." All this took place to fulfill what had been spoken by the

Lord through the prophet: "Look, the virgin shall conceive and bear a son, and they shall name him Emmanuel," which means, "God is with us." When Joseph awoke from sleep, he did as the angel of the Lord commanded him; he took her as his wife, but had no marital relations with her until she had borne a son; and he named him Jesus. (Matthew 1:18-25)

In the sixth month the angel Gabriel was sent by God to a town in Galilee called Nazareth, to a virgin engaged to a man whose name was Joseph, of the house of David. The virgin's name was Mary. And he came to her and said, "Greetings, favored one! The Lord is with you." But she was much perplexed by his words and pondered what sort of greeting this might be. The angel said to her, "Do not be afraid, Mary, for you have found favor with God. And now, you will conceive in your womb and bear a son, and you will name him Jesus. He will be great, and will be called the Son of the Most High, and God will give to him the throne of his ancestor David. He will reign over the house of Jacob forever, and of his kingdom there will be no end." Mary said to the angel, "How can this be, since I am a virgin?" The angel said to her, "The Holy Spirit will come upon you, and the power of the Most High will overshadow you; therefore the child to be born will be holy; he will be called Son of God. And now, your relative Elizabeth in her old age has also conceived a son; and this is the sixth month for her who was said to be barren. For nothing will be impossible with God." Then Mary said, "Here am I, the servant of the Lord;

let it be with me according to your word." Then the angel departed from her.

And Mary said, "My soul magnifies the Lord, and my spirit rejoices in God my Savior, for he has looked with favor on the lowliness of his servant. Surely from now on all generations will call me blessed; for the Mighty One has done great things for me, and holy is his name. His mercy is for those who fear him from generation to generation . . . . "

All went to their towns to be registered. Joseph also went from the town of Nazareth in Galilee to Judea, to the city of David called Bethlehem, because he was descended from the house and family of David. He went to be registered with Mary, to whom he was engaged and who was expecting a child. While they were there, the time came for her to deliver her child. And she gave birth to her firstborn son and wrapped him in bands of cloth, and laid him in a manger, because there was no place for them in the inn. (Luke 1:26-48; 2:3-7)

On the third day there was a wedding in Cana of Galilee, and the mother of Jesus was there. Jesus and his disciples had also been invited to the wedding. When the wine gave out, the mother of Jesus said to him, "They have no wine." And Jesus said to her, "Woman, what concern is that to you and to me? My hour has not yet come." His mother said to the servants, "Do whatever he tells you." (John 2:1-5)

Meanwhile, standing near the cross of Jesus were his mother, and his mother's sister, Mary the wife of Clopas, and Mary Magdalene. When Jesus saw his mother and the disciple whom he loved standing beside her, he said to his mother, "Woman, here is your son." Then he said to the disciple, "Here is your mother." And from this hour the disciple took her into his own home. (John 19:25-27)

Mary's story appears in the gospels of Matthew, Luke, and John, with brief mentions in the gospel of Mark. In both the Luke and Matthew versions, Mary becomes pregnant, but not from relations with her eventual husband, Joseph. She is described as a virgin who conceives with the help of the Holy Spirit. In Matthew's gospel, an angel intervenes with this news just as Joseph is ready 'to dismiss her quietly' so she will not be exposed to public disgrace.

In Luke's gospel, Mary learns of her pregnancy from the angel Gabriel, who visits her after she is engaged to Joseph of the historic house of David. The angel calls Mary 'favored one' and tells her that she will conceive and bear a son whom she will name Jesus. Not possible, says Mary, the virgin. The angel assures her the conception will occur, and the child to be born will be holy. Gabriel reminds Mary that her cousin Elizabeth has miraculously conceived in old age. How can she be pregnant, Mary asks, since she is a virgin? She is told that the Holy Spirit will come upon her, and the power of the Most High will overshadow her. Mary then accepts her role, "Let it be with me, according to your word" (Luke 1:38).

She travels immediately to her cousin's home to talk these things over with Elizabeth. And communicate they do; dramatically and powerfully; Mary's very presence and greeting causes the child in

Elizabeth's womb to leap for joy. Mary answers in song, known as the "Magnificat," rejoicing in God and the great things God does–showing strength, scattering the proud, bringing down the powerful, lifting up the lowly, filling the hungry, fulfilling the promises made to their ancestors.

Through her first trimester, Mary remains in the home of Elizabeth. Subsequently, continuing the Luke story, she and Joseph go to Bethlehem to register according to the edict of Emperor Augustus. The biblical narrative does not describe the actual birthplace, but given the difficulties of labor and delivery in even the most comfortable of circumstances, it seems likely that Mary faced challenges in the birthing. Unable to find accommodation in an inn, she gives birth and lays her child in a trough where animals feed.

After eight days, the baby is circumcised and named Jesus. Mary and Joseph then take him to Jerusalem for presentation in the temple. While there, they encounter two prophets who confirm Jesus' destiny. The first is a man named Simeon to whom it had been revealed that he would not die before he had seen the Messiah. When Mary and Joseph bring in Jesus, Simeon takes the child in his arms and praises God, saying that his eyes have seen salvation and "a light for revelation to the Gentiles and for glory to your people Israel" (Luke 2:30-32).

Their second dramatic meeting is with the prophet Anna, a woman who never leaves the premises, but worships at the temple day and night. She praises God and speaks about the child "to all who were looking for the redemption of Jerusalem" (Luke 2:36-38).

When Jesus is twelve, Mary and Joseph take him again to Jerusalem for the festival of the Passover. At the festival's end, they begin their journey home with a group of travelers, unaware that Jesus has stayed behind. They start to look for him among family and friends, but cannot find him and go back to Jerusalem to search. Three days later, they finally find him in the temple, interacting with the teachers and amazing all who hear him. Mary accurately points out that he's caused his parents considerable anxiety, but he reassures her that he needs to be in God's house. They go home to Nazareth where Mary "treasured all these things in her heart" (Luke 2:51).

Mary's story continues in John's gospel where she appears at both the beginning and ending of Jesus' ministry. When the wine runs out at the Cana wedding, it is Jesus' mother who says that "they have no wine" (John 2:3), leading to Jesus' first miracle, the turning of water into wine. Mary's final vision of her son is when he is dying in a cruel governmental execution. From the cross of crucifixion, Jesus sees his mother standing next to "the disciple that he loved" and says to her, "Woman, here is your son." And to the disciple, "here is your mother" (John 19:25-27). We are told that Jesus' disciple takes Mary into his home.

In the Book of Acts, Mary remains involved with Jesus' community. "All these were constantly devoting themselves to prayer, together with certain women, including Mary the mother of Jesus, as well as his brothers" (Acts 1:14). Like the other stories of Advent women, Mary's life continues in our imaginings. Whatever the cultural and political challenges, these faithful women show us—each in her own way, time, and circumstance—that there is always a new path, fresh and hopeful.

Symbols: Mother with child, pregnant woman with female friend, woman with baby in manger, icon of Mary

Questions for Reflections:

What is Mary's cultural status?

What do we learn from the biblical narratives about her relationship to Joseph? To Elizabeth?

Why does Mary sing?

What do we learn from Mary about mothering? About friendship?

Why did Mary stay with Elizabeth for three months? What is your idea of that experience for both women—what did they do and talk about every day?

How would you describe the birthing scene?

Why does the gospel of John place Mary in the Cana wedding story? At the foot of the cross?

What do we learn about Mary's *feelings* from the biblical narratives?

How is Mary a woman of Advent?

REFERENCES

Harrelson, W.J. (Ed). (2003). *The New Interpreter's Study Bible.* Abingdon Press.

Hyman, P.E., & Ofer, D. (Eds). *Jewish Women: A Comprehensive Historical Encyclopedia.* Retrieved from www.jwa.org.

Meyers, C. (Ed). (2001). *Women in Scripture.* Eerdmans.